RECTANGLE PIZZAZZ

Fast, Fun & Finished in a Day

Judy Sisneros

C&T PUBLISHING

TEXT COPYRIGHT © 2008 BY JUDY SISNEROS

ARTWORK COPYRIGHT © 2008 BY C&T PUBLISHING, INC.

Publisher: Amy Marson

Editorial Director: Gailen Runge

Acquisitions Editor: Jan Grigsby

Editors: Karla Menaugh and Kesel Wilson

Technical Editors: Susan Nelsen and Nanette Zeller

Copyeditor/Proofreader: Wordfirm Inc.

Cover Designer/Design Director: Kristen Yenche

Junior Designer: Kiera Lofgreen

Production Coordinator: Kirstie L. Pettersen

Illustrators: Kirstie L. Pettersen and Joshua A. Mulks

Photography by C&T Publishing, Inc., unless otherwise noted

Published by C&T Publishing, Inc., P.O. Box 1456, Lafayette, CA 94549

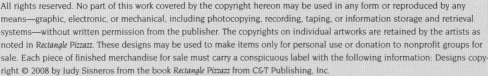

Library of Congress Cataloging-in-Publication Data

Sisneros, Judy,

  Rectangle pizzazz : fast, fun & finished in a day / Judy Sisneros.

    p. cm.

  ISBN-13: 978-1-57120-446-2 (paper trade : alk. paper)

  ISBN-10: 1-57120-446-6 (paper trade : alk. paper)

  1. Patchwork--Patterns. 2. Quilting--Patterns. I. Title.

  TT835.S554455 2008

  746.46'041--dc22

                        2007020444

Printed in China

10 9 8 7 6 5 4 3 2 1

CONTENTS

DEDICATION

THIS BOOK IS DEDICATED TO my beautiful daughters, Tracey and Donna. Their love and support have never wavered.

ACKNOWLEDGMENTS

SPECIAL THANKS TO THE FOLLOWING companies for their contributions of fabric and notions: Benartex, Trendtex Fabrics, Michael Miller Fabrics, Kona Bay Fabrics, Superior Threads, Fairfield Processing (Batting), and Olfa. Thanks to Sharon Malachowski for her assistance in machine quilting — I couldn't have done it all myself. Also, thanks to the staff at C&T Publishing, especially my Editors, Karla Menaugh and Kesel Wilson.

INTRODUCTION

MANY QUILTERS ARE BUSY PEOPLE who want to make something that is **fast, fun, and finished**, but still beautiful and exciting. My previous book, *9-Patch Pizzazz: Fast Fun, & Finished in a Day*, published by C&T Publishing in 2006, contained Nine-Patch quilts that were easy and fun to create. The response from readers was amazing.

But one can make only so many Nine Patches, so I began looking for something different. What about rectangles? They are among the most basic of shapes but can be incorporated into a quilt in many different ways. When you work with rectangles, the possibilities are endless, there are no points to match, and you can make rectangles any size. One of my new projects has only two sizes of rectangles, no other shapes. Other projects combine rectangles and curves, rectangles and bars, and rectangles on point. Most are beginner friendly, but the challenge of choosing the right fabrics makes these projects fun for everyone.

So, get out the most beautiful fabrics in your stash, put a new blade in your rotary cutter, and let's go.

The Fabric Does the Work

WHEN PEOPLE LOOK AT A QUILT, what do they notice first? The fabric. Even the impact of a fabulous design depends on the fabric choices being fabulous as well. And even a simple quilt can be absolutely wonderful if you use great fabric.

When I began teaching, I was surprised at how many students wanted to make an exact copy of my sample quilt. Unfortunately, many fabric manufacturers do not reprint designs, so you may not be able to exactly reproduce the quilts in this book. But the designs will be wonderful even if you can't duplicate my fabric choices. My goal is to help you use these techniques to make quilts that will reflect *your* interests and favorite fabrics.

The fabrics available now are incredible. You can find any style and design you can imagine. I tried to use many different fabrics—large-scale prints, tone-on-tone fabrics, batiks, Asian designs, and others. Large-scale prints are definitely my favorite. Because the fabrics are so beautiful, the quilts look much more involved than they really are. I am including directions for various quilt sizes in some projects so you can try a wallhanging, lap quilt, or bed quilt.

Choosing Fabrics

All of the quilts in this book use at least one fabulous focus print and several companion fabrics. Usually, I choose a focus fabric containing several different colors and companion fabrics to complement that fabric.

The focus fabric is the star of the quilt and the coordinating fabrics are the supporting actors. The star is much better looking with the right supporting fabrics. Choosing the right fabric can be exciting and fun, but also a bit scary.

Examples of good fabric combinations

Here is one of my most important rules: If the fabric doesn't add to the quilt, it doesn't play. No matter how beautiful the fabric, if it doesn't enhance the focus fabric or the overall design, I don't use it. I also do not use solid fabrics—ever. Even if a fabric looks like a solid, you can be sure it's a tone-on-tone if it's in one of my quilts. In my opinion, solid colors look flat in a quilt.

Be sure that you balance busy prints with more restful ones. The tone-on-tone fabrics bring out colors but don't overwhelm the overall effect. If you use only busy prints, the viewer's eye doesn't know where to focus on the quilt and has no place to rest.

Too busy

Color Is Your Friend

Color is one of the first elements people notice in a quilt. If you use mostly blue fabrics, people will talk about your "blue" quilt. If you use colors that you love, you will be more likely to love the quilt you make. A basic color wheel is a good tool to help you decide on color use in your quilt. There are many good books available on color, such as *Visual Coloring* by Joen Wolfrom or the *3-in-1 Color Tool*, both from C&T Publishing.

Warm colors include red-violet, red, red-orange, orange, yellow-orange, and yellow. Cool colors include violet, blue-violet, blue, blue-green, green, and yellow-green. Remember that a little yellow goes a long way. If you use a dark focus fabric, try to use at least one lighter companion fabric to bring out one of the colors in the focus fabric.

Good match of green fabrics

A companion fabric brings out the color in a dark focus fabric.

When you choose companion fabrics, be sure that you select similar variations of the colors from the focus fabric. If it's a blue-green in the focus fabric, it also should be a blue-green in the companion fabric.

The green looks out of place with the focus fabric.

TOOLS TO MAKE YOUR TASK EASIER

WOULDN'T IT BE WONDERFUL if we all had a large studio with a lovely view, nearby powder room, stocked refrigerator, and huge design wall? I have seen several studios that fit this description, but mine is not one of them. My studio is a bedroom measuring 11′ × 11′; it's the best I can do in a small condo. Some quilters have only the use of a corner in the den or the dining room table, but we all can make beautiful quilts in whatever space we have.

Sewing machine in good working order

Clean your sewing machine and replace the needle regularly. The features I most appreciate are the needle-down and knee-lift options. Many of the newer machines have a $\frac{1}{4}''$ foot with a ledge so you can't sew a wider seam—a great tool. If your machine is not in a cabinet, a table-top extension is a must.

Good light

In the daytime, work with the blinds open. At night, use enough light so you can see your work clearly. Usually it's best to make fabric choices in natural light.

Foamcore board

Found at office supply stores, foamcore makes a lightweight, portable design surface. You can purchase it in 4´ × 8´ sheets and cover it with white felt, fleece, or batting and then staple it to a wall for permanent use. I use foamcore measuring about 32″ × 40″ for smaller projects. You can easily take this size to workshops. If you don't have a wall to which you can attach it permanently, you can store it behind a door when you are not using it. After you get your design on the wall, stand back and look at it from across the room. This perspective lets you see the full effect of the design. It's harder to get the full effect if you design on a table or the floor.

Rotary cutter and mat

It's a good idea to have a cutting mat that measures at least 24″. When you fold fabric selvage-to-selvage, it will fit neatly on your cutting mat so you can cut strips easily. Be sure to clean your rotary cutter and change the blades regularly. Also carefully note how you take the rotary cutter apart, so you can put it back together properly. It works much better that way.

Cutting surface

If you can raise your cutting surface, your back will thank you. I put PVC pipe on the legs of a six-foot table to raise it to a comfortable height.

Needles and thread

There are so many wonderful threads and needles on the market today. Neutral thread works well when sewing projects with various colors. I usually use 100% cotton thread, but some of the new lint-free polyester threads are terrific too. Choose the needle type you prefer and remember to change the needle regularly.

Basic sewing supplies

SHARP SCISSORS used for fabric only

SEAM RIPPER (Yes, you may make a mistake!)

ROUND-HEAD PINS and **MAGNETIC PINCUSHION**

RULERS: $6\frac{1}{2}''$ square, $12\frac{1}{2}''$ square, 6″ × 24″ rectangle (These are the ones I consider essential.)

 **hint** If you have used the same seam ripper for years, buy a new one. They don't stay sharp forever.

TO THE NINES

Jungle Pizzazz, 54″ × 72″, Judy Sisneros, 2003.

Several years ago, I designed a quilt for a class at a local quilt shop. The class was to be held the day before an annual outdoor quilt show. It was the ninth year of the show and the ninth year that I had taught the day before the show and the date was August 9. So, the shop owner wanted me to develop a class around the number nine. Quite a challenge! I came up with this design using nine fabrics—the quilt has nine blocks across and nine blocks down, but it's not square, and it takes about nine hours to complete (really!). The class was a great success, and the quilt was very popular. Since then I have made this design as a wallhanging and in twin, double, and queen sizes.

	WALLHANGING *54″ × 72″* (See *Garden Party* on page 39.)	**TWIN** *72″ × 96″* (See *Surfer's Delight* on page 40.)	**DOUBLE** *78″ × 96″* (See *Alyson's Aloha* on page 40.)	**QUEEN** *96″ × 104″* (See *Flaming Iris* on page 41.)
FABRIC REQUIREMENTS (YARDAGE IS BASED ON 42″-WIDE FABRIC.)				
Focus fabric	**One Focus Fabric** $2^1/2$ yards (includes binding)	**Three Focus Fabrics** FABRICS 1 AND 2: $1^3/8$ yards each **PLUS** FABRIC 3: $2^1/4$ yards (includes binding)	**One Focus Fabric** $4^1/2$ yards (includes binding) **OR** **Three Focus Fabrics** FABRICS 1 AND 2: $1^3/8$ yards each FABRIC 3: $2^1/4$ yards (includes binding)	**One Focus Fabric** $5^1/2$ yards (includes binding)
Companion fabrics	**8 prints:** $1/3$ yard each	**8 prints:** $5/8$ yard each	**8 prints:** $5/8$ yard each **OR** **12 prints:** $1/2$ yard each	**8 prints:** $3/4$ yard each
Backing	$3^1/3$ yards	$5^2/3$ yards	$5^2/3$ yards	$8^1/2$ yards
Batting	60″ × 78″	78″ × 102″	84″ × 102″	102″ × 110″
CUTTING INSTRUCTIONS (WOF = WIDTH OF FABRIC)				
Focus fabric	**Cut 7 strips $8^1/2″$ × wof.** **Subcut into:** 39 rectangles $6^1/2″ × 8^1/2″$ 6 rectangles $2^1/2″ × 8^1/2″$ **Cut 7 strips $2^1/2″$ × wof** (for binding).	**From Fabrics 1–3,** **cut 5 strips $8^1/2″$ × wof.** **Subcut each into:** 23 rectangles $6^1/2″ × 8^1/2″$ 2 rectangles $4^1/2″ × 8^1/2″$ 2 rectangles $2^1/2″ × 8^1/2″$ (You'll have extra pieces for fabric choices.) **From Fabric 3,** **cut 9 strips $2^1/2″$ × wof** (for binding).	**For 1-fabric option,** **cut 13 strips $8^1/2″$ × wof.** **Subcut into:** 77 rectangles $6^1/2″ × 8^1/2″$ 8 rectangles $2^1/2″ × 8^1/2″$ **OR** **For 3-fabric option, cut 5 strips $8^1/2″$ × wof from Fabrics 1–3.** **Subcut each into:** 26 rectangles $6^1/2″ × 8^1/2″$ 3 rectangles $2^1/2″ × 8^1/2″$ (You'll have an extra piece for color placement options.) **For either option (use Fabric 3 for the 3-fabric option), cut 10 strips $2^1/2″$ × wof** (for binding).	**Cut 18 strips $8^1/2″$ × wof.** **Subcut into:** 100 rectangles $6^1/2″ × 8^1/2″$ (If making cutout at foot of bed, you will need only 95 of these rectangles.) 4 rectangles $4^1/2″ × 8^1/2″$ (Cutout needs only 3.) 4 rectangles $2^1/2″ × 8^1/2″$ (Cutout needs only 3.) **Cut 11 strips $2^1/2″$ × wof** (for binding).
Companion fabrics	**From each fabric,** **cut 2 strips $4^1/2″$ × wof.** **Subcut into:** 256 rectangles $2^1/2″ × 4^1/2″$ (You'll only need 240; the extra can be used for color placement options.)	**From each fabric,** **cut 4 strips $4^1/2″$ × wof.** **Subcut into:** 512 rectangles $2^1/2″ × 4^1/2″$ (You'll only need 432; the extra can be used for color placement.)	**For 8-fabric option: From each fabric, cut 4 strips $4^1/2″$ × wof.** **Subcut into:** 512 rectangles $2^1/2″ × 4^1/2″$ (You'll only need 464; the extra can be used for color placement.) If using more than 8 fabrics, cut a total of 32 strips $4^1/2″$ × wof.	**From each fabric,** **cut 5 strips $4^1/2″$ × wof.** **Subcut into:** 640 rectangles $2^1/2″ × 4^1/2″$ (You'll only need 624; the extra can be used for color placement.)

Fabric Requirements and Cutting Instructions

Begin with a wonderful, multicolored, large-scale print for the focus fabric. Choose 8 fabrics to coordinate with the focus fabric, using the various colors in the print. Try to use all the colors if possible. You can see variations on *To the Nines* on pages 39–41. Alternate fabric selection combinations are given in the chart on the previous page.

note

If your focus fabric has people, animals, or other figures that you want to fussy cut, you can alternate cutting the 2½˝ strips for use in the binding with cutting the 8½˝ strips. Do **not** decapitate the animals or people in the print. It's OK to cut off legs and wings, but not heads.

If your fabric is directional, make sure the design is upright.

Sewing the Rectangles

1. Stack the 2½˝ × 4½˝ companion fabric rectangles, placing each fabric in a separate stack on your sewing machine table.

Stacks are ready to sew.

2. A design note here: Be aware that some fabrics may not work well side-by-side, so don't put these fabrics next to each other in the quilt. The next steps will tell you how many pairs and combinations you will need.

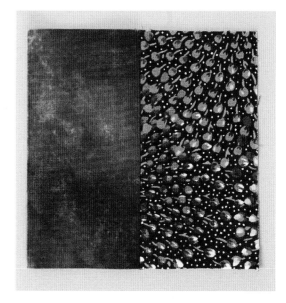

These fabrics are OK side-by-side.

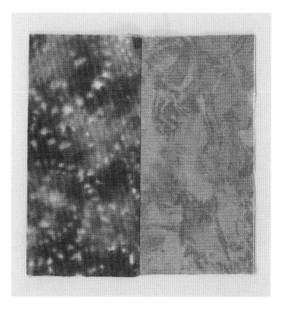

These fabrics should not be side-by-side.

3. For the twin- and queen-size quilts only, first sew two 2½″ × 4½″ rectangles together as shown below, selecting compatible fabric combinations. Make 4 pairs for the twin- and queen-size quilts. These are for the endings of some of the rows in the layouts. Set these aside.

Make 4 pairs for the twin- or queen-size quilt.

4. For all quilt sizes, sew rectangles in pairs, using compatible fabric combinations. Seam these rectangles along the 4½″ edges of the rectangles. Chain piece as you sew. Use as much variety as possible in making the fabric combinations for the pairs. You need 84 pairs for the wallhanging, 144 pairs for the twin size, 160 pairs for the double size, and 208 pairs for the queen size. Sometimes I don't make all of the pairs until I've started assembling them into sets, so I can see which colors I need to balance the design.

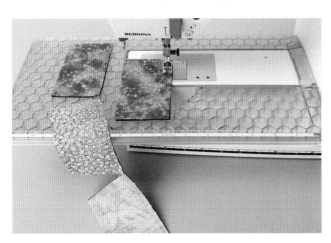

Chain piece the rectangles.

5. Use the pairs from Step 4 to make the set shown below. Make 6 sets for the wallhanging, 4 for the twin size, 8 for the double size, and 4 for the queen size. These are for the beginnings and endings of some of the rows in the layouts. Set these sets aside.

Sew pairs together in sets.

6. Sew a third rectangle to each of the remaining pairs from Step 4, being careful not to sew 2 rectangles of the same fabrics together. Press the seams to one side.

7. Sew 2 units from Step 6 together to make the block shown below. Make 36 blocks for the wallhanging, 68 blocks for the twin size, 72 blocks for the double size, and 100 blocks for the queen size.

Sew sections together.

hint When you sew the units together, be sure to press the seams in one unit in the opposite direction from the seams in the other unit.

8. Locate your quilt size on the quilt assembly diagram below. The coloring in the diagram will be especially helpful if you used 3 focus fabrics in your project. Lay out the focus fabric pieces and the rectangle units as needed for your project size. If your focus fabric is directional, be sure it is oriented correctly and make sure that matching fabrics are not side-by-side from row to row. The gray corners in the diagram indicate the sections to omit for corner cutouts for the *queen size* (optional). Sew each row together and then join the rows. Press.

Bed sizes can vary owing to the thickness of the mattress. Adjust the size of your quilt as needed, remembering that a block is 6″ wide and 8″ long.

Gray blocks show corner cutouts for queen size.

Assembly diagram for quilt sizes

CURVES AROUND THE RECTANGLE

Geisha Delight, 42˝ × 54˝, Judy Sisneros, 2007.

Some of the most beautiful panel fabrics are on the market today—and many quilters buy them but have no idea how to use them, or see them but don't buy them, for the same reason.

Large-scale fabrics fascinate me, and I love to use them in fun ways. For this project, start with a rectangle cut from a gorgeous panel or large-scale print. Add blocks with gradual curves to create a quilt with beauty and movement. The most difficult part of making this design is sewing the curved blocks, but even that is not too difficult. The rest of the quilt consists of rectangles. No points to match!

Fabric Requirements

(Yardage is based on 42″-wide fabric.)

This project uses a 12½″ × 24½″ rectangle panel, but instructions are also given for a 12½″ × 18½″ rectangle. Any size rectangle will work, as long as the dimensions can be divided by 6 plus a ½″ seam allowance. Try one of those panels you bought but haven't used yet.

FOCUS FABRIC: 12½″ × 24½″ rectangle

NAVY: 1¼ yards for curved blocks and Rail Fence blocks

RUST: 1½ yards for curved blocks, Rail Fence blocks, and binding

PRINT: ⅞ yard for inner border and Rail Fence blocks

BACKING: 2⅔ yards

BATTING: 48″ × 60″

Cutting Instructions

(wof = width of fabric)

FROM THE NAVY FABRIC, CUT:

3 strips 6″ × wof

4 strips 2½″ × wof

2 squares 6⅞″ × 6⅞″

FROM THE RUST FABRIC, CUT:

3 strips 6″ × wof

9 strips 2½″ × wof (save 5 strips for binding)

2 squares 6⅞″ × 6⅞″

FROM THE PRINT FABRIC, CUT:

4 strips 3½″ × wof

Subcut into:
2 strips 3½″ × 36½″
2 strips 3½″ × 30½″

4 strips 2½″ × wof

Sewing the Curved Blocks

1. Place a 6″-wide strip of navy fabric, folded in half widthwise with selvages aligned, over a 6″-wide strip of rust fabric, also folded in half and overlapping 3″ as shown. Align the folded edges of the strips.

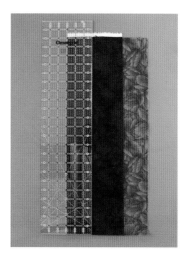

Overlap 2 strips.

2. Place a ruler on the strips as shown. The ruler helps you see where the fabric underneath ends. Draw a line with gradual curves similar to the line in the photograph, staying within the overlapped area. Starting at the fold, slowly and carefully cut gradual curves across the overlapped strips. Begin by cutting at least 1″ straight in **before** beginning the curve. The curve should be gradual.

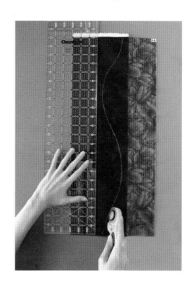

Cutting the gradual curve

3. Separate the 2 fabrics and remove the excess fabric as shown.

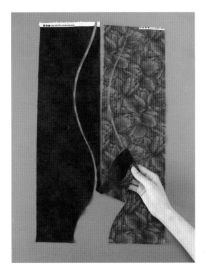

Remove the small sections.

4. Unfold the strips. Fit the 2 strips together side-by-side, wrong sides up. Mark across both fabrics every 1½" along the length of the strips.

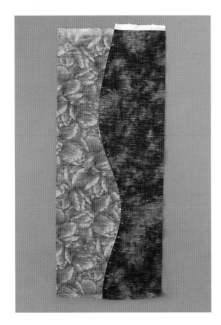

Mark the strips as shown.

5. Carefully pin the strips at the marks, right sides together as shown.

Pin the strips.

6. Stitch and then press toward the navy fabric. Be sure there are no puckers.

7. Cut the finished strips into 6½" squares, positioning the ruler so that the curve does not fall in the same place in each block. This gives variety to the blocks. You will get six 6½" curved blocks from each strip.

8. Repeat Steps 1–7 to make 2 more strip sets for additional curved blocks. You need a total of 16 blocks.

That was the **hard** part.
Now let's do the **easy** part.

Sewing the Rail Fence and Corner Blocks

RAIL FENCE BLOCK A

1. Sew a 2½″ strip of navy fabric to a 2½″ strip of rust fabric.

2. Add a 2½″ strip of print fabric to the **rust** side of the strip set. Press.

3. Cut 6 blocks, 6½″ square.

BLOCK A—Cut 6.

RAIL FENCE BLOCK B

1. Sew a 2½″ strip of navy fabric to a 2½″ strip of print fabric.

2. Cut off 15″ of the strip set from Step 1 and set it aside for use in Block C.

3. Cut 15″ from a 2½″ strip of rust fabric and set it aside for use in Block C.

4. Add the remaining piece of the 2½″ strip of rust fabric to the **navy** side of the remaining piece of the strip set from Step 1. Press.

5. Repeat Steps 1–4 to make a second strip set, using the full length of each strip.

6. Cut 10 blocks, 6½″ square.

BLOCK B—Cut 10.

RAIL FENCE BLOCK C

1. Sew a 2½″ strip of rust fabric to a 2½″ strip of print fabric.

2. Add a 2½″ strip of navy fabric to the **print** side of the strip set. Press.

3. Make another navy/print/rust strip set using the 15″ pieces set aside from Block B.

4. Cut a total of 8 blocks, 6½″ square.

BLOCK C—Cut 8.

CORNER BLOCKS

1. Cut the 6⅞" squares of rust and navy fabrics in half diagonally to make 2 triangles from each square.

2. Sew 4 rust triangles to 4 navy triangles to make 4 corner blocks. Press toward the navy fabric.

Corner blocks

Quilt Assembly

1. Place the blocks on your design surface. Noting the color placement in the quilt assembly diagram, arrange 2 curved blocks for the top of the focus fabric rectangle, and 2 curved blocks for the bottom of the rectangle. Sew the curved blocks to the rectangle. Press.

2. Sew 2 rows together for the sides of the rectangle, each containing 6 curved blocks. Again, note the color placement. Sew one row to each side of the rectangle. Press toward the center.

3. Sew the 2 print 3½" × 36½" strips to the sides of the center section. Press. Then add the 3½" × 30½" print strips to the top and bottom of the center section. Press toward the print strip.

The inner border measurement of 3″ finished equals half of a 6″ block. Therefore, the math for the next row is still based on 6″ increments. Two 3″ finished borders (1 on each side) equals a 6″ block.

4. Place the Rail Fence blocks around the quilt as shown. Note the placement for Blocks A, B, and C in each row. Sew 7 Rail Fence blocks together for each side. Attach the units to the sides of the quilt.

5. Attach corner blocks to the top and bottom Rail Fence rows and sew the rows to the quilt as shown in the quilt assembly diagram.

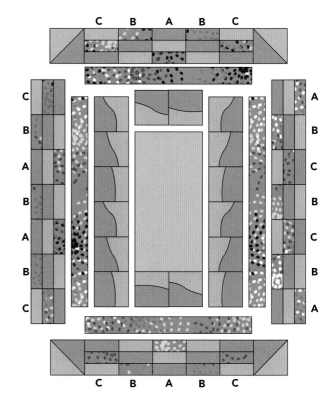

Quilt assembly diagram

	MINI-WALLHANGING	WALLHANGING
	$32^1/2'' \times 38^1/2''$ (See *Butterfly Garden* on page 41.)	$42'' \times 48''$ (See *Wisteria in Bloom* on page 42.) The curved blocks around the rectangle have high contrast color. Then a 3″ finished border of focus fabric is added so it blends in. The outer border of blocks is also made from the curved blocks, using focus fabric and black.

FABRIC REQUIREMENTS (YARDAGE IS BASED ON 42″-WIDE FABRIC.)

Focus fabric or panel	$12^1/2'' \times 18^1/2''$ rectangle	$2^1/4$ yards (includes center rectangle)
Coordinating fabric	$^5/8$ yard for curved blocks and corners	NA
Light fabric	$^5/8$ yard for curved blocks and narrow border	$^5/8$ yard for curved blocks around rectangle
Dark fabric	$^7/8$ yard for outer border and binding	$1^1/2$ yards for outer curved blocks and binding
Backing	$1^1/8$ yards	$2^3/4$ yards
Batting	$38'' \times 44''$	$48'' \times 54''$

CUTTING INSTRUCTIONS (WOF = WIDTH OF FABRIC)

Focus fabric or panel	$12^1/2'' \times 18^1/2''$ rectangle	Cut 1 rectangle $12^1/2'' \times 18^1/2''$.
		Cut 7 strips 6″ × wof.
		Cut 4 strips $3^1/2'' \times$ wof.
		Subcut into:
		    2 strips $3^1/2'' \times 36^1/2''$
		    2 strips $3^1/2'' \times 24^1/2''$

Coordinating fabric	Cut 1 strip $6^1/2'' \times$ wof. Subcut into: 4 squares $6^1/2'' \times 6^1/2''$ Cut 2 strips 6″ × wof.	NA

Light fabric	Cut 2 strips 6″ × wof.
	Cut 4 strips $1^3/4'' \times$ wof.
	Subcut into:
	    2 strips $1^3/4'' \times 30^1/2''$
	    2 strips $1^3/4'' \times 27''$
		Cut 3 strips 6″ × wof.

Dark fabric	Cut 4 strips $3^1/2'' \times$ wof.
	Subcut into:
	    2 strips $3^1/2'' \times 39''$
	    2 strips $3^1/2'' \times 27''$
	Cut 4 strips $2^1/2'' \times$ wof (for binding).
		Cut 1 strip $6^1/2'' \times$ wof.
		Subcut into:
		    4 squares $6^1/2'' \times 6^1/2''$
		Cut 4 strips 6″ × wof.
		Cut 5 strips $2^1/2'' \times$ wof (for binding).

QUILT ASSEMBLY

	1. Make 10 curved blocks, following the directions on pages 17–18, using 6″ coordinating fabric and 6″ light fabric strips. **2.** Sew 2 curved blocks to the top and bottom of the center rectangle, noting color placement. Press. Sew 3 curved blocks together for each side. Add $6^1/2''$ corner squares to the ends of the rows and sew them to the sides. Press. **3.** Sew $1^3/4'' \times 30^1/2''$ strips of light fabric to each side of the quilt. Press. **4.** Sew a $1^3/4'' \times 27''$ light strip to a $3^1/2'' \times 27''$ strip of dark fabric. Press. Sew to the top of the quilt, noting color placement. Press. Repeat for the bottom of the quilt. **5.** Sew a $3^1/2'' \times 39''$ strip of dark fabric to each side of the quilt. Press.	**1.** Make 14 curved blocks, following the directions on pages 17–18, using 6″ focus fabric and 6″ light fabric strips for the rows around the rectangle. **2.** Sew 2 curved blocks to the top and bottom of the center rectangle. Sew a row of 5 blocks to each side of the quilt, noting color placement. Press. **3.** Sew $3^1/2'' \times 24^1/2''$ strips of focus fabric to the top and bottom and sew $3^1/2'' \times 36^1/2''$ strips of focus fabric to each side. Press. **4.** Make 22 curved blocks, following the instructions on pages 17–18, using 6″ focus fabric and 6″ dark fabric strips. **5.** Stitch 2 rows of 5 dark curved blocks to add to the top and bottom, noting color placement. Press. **6.** Sew together 2 rows of 6 dark curved blocks. Then add a dark $6^1/2''$ square to the ends of each row. Sew these rows to the sides of the quilt. Press.

Other Options

QUILTS WITH 12½″ × 18½″ CENTERS

To create stunning quilts like *Butterfly Garden*, *Wisteria in Bloom*, and *Geisha* (pages 41–42), make the curved blocks in the same manner as for the featured quilt. Just change the number of blocks and the borders.

> ## note
> You could use a horizontal rather than a vertical rectangle. To see the placement, turn the diagram on its side.

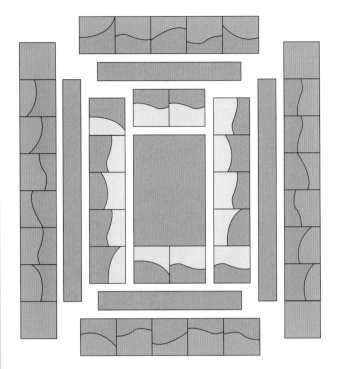

Wallhanging quilt assembly diagram

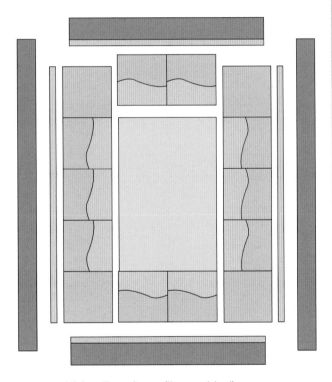

Mini-wallhanging quilt assembly diagram

Close-up of *Geisha*

RECTANGLES ON POINT

Floral Fantasia, 54″ × 66″, Judy Sisneros, 2007. Machine quilted by Sharon Malachowski, Sebastopol, California.

It's amazing to me how different a quilt can look if you put the blocks on point. This project uses 8½″ × 12½″ rectangles, 6½″ × 8½″ rectangles, and square blocks, with a few odd sizes thrown in to make everything fit. The biggest challenge for me in designing the quilt was calculating the size of the setting triangles. I think the result was worth the effort. I made two of these—one with Asian fabrics and this one with a fabulous floral. Any beautiful, multicolored fabric will work as long as it looks good on point. *Cranes in Flight*, the quilt made with Asian fabrics, is shown on page 43.

Fabric Requirements

(Yardage is based on 42″-wide fabric.)

FLORAL FOCUS FABRIC: 2 yards

PURPLE: 1⅞ yards for blocks and setting triangles

TURQUOISE: ⅝ yard for blocks

STRIPED: ¾ yard for blocks and binding

BACKING: 3⅓ yards

BATTING: 60″ × 72″

Cutting Instructions

(wof = width of fabric)

Label the pieces A–K as you cut them. The quilt assembly diagram (page 26) shows the lettering to help you with the design layout.

FROM THE FLORAL FOCUS FABRIC, CUT:

5 strips 8½″ × wof

Subcut into:

13 rectangles 8½″ × 12½″ (A)

2 strips 6½″ × wof

Subcut into:

8 rectangles 6½″ × 8½″ (B)

2 squares 6½″ × 6½″ (C)

FROM THE PURPLE FABRIC, CUT:

6 strips 2½″ × wof

Subcut 4 strips into:

16 rectangles 2½″ × 8½″ (D)

Save the 2 remaining strips to make the block center units.

3 strips 6½″ × wof

Subcut into:

2 rectangles 6½″ × 12½″ (E)

2 rectangles 6½″ × 10½″ (F)

2 rectangles 6½″ × 8½″ (G)

4 rectangles 6½″ × 4½″ (H)

4 rectangles 6½″ × 2½″ (I)

1 strip 12¼″ × wof

Subcut into:

1 square 12¼″ × 12¼″; then cut diagonally once for 2 triangles (J)

Cut diagonally once.

1 square 9¾″ × 9¾″; then cut diagonally twice for 4 triangles (K)

Cut diagonally twice.

1 square 9½″ × 9½″; then cut diagonally once for 2 triangles (L)

1 strip 9¾″ × wof

Subcut into:

4 squares 9¾″ × 9¾″; then cut diagonally twice for 16 triangles (K). With the K triangles you already cut, you will have a total of 20, but you need only 18.

FROM THE TURQUOISE FABRIC, CUT:

6 strips 2½″ × wof

Subcut 4 strips into:

16 rectangles 2½″ × 8½″ (M)

Save the remaining 2 strips to make the block center units.

FROM THE STRIPED FABRIC, CUT:

8 strips 2½″ × wof (save 7 strips for binding)

Sewing the Blocks

1. Sew a 2½˝ striped strip to a 2½˝ purple strip. Add a turquoise strip so the striped strip is in the middle. Press the seams in one direction. Cut the strip set in half. Each piece should be about 21˝ long.

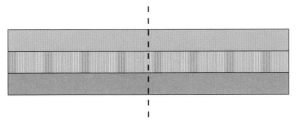

Cut strip set in half.

2. Cut 1 purple 2½˝ strip and 1 turquoise 2½˝ strip in half. Each piece should be approximately 21˝ long.

3. Sew 1 purple strip to the turquoise edge of 1 3-part strip set from Step 1 to make a 4-part strip set with purple strips on both outer edges. Press. Cut the strip set into eight 2½˝ sections.

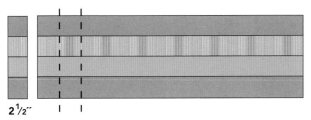

2½˝

Cut into 8 sections.

4. Sew 2 purple D rectangles to each section from Step 3 as shown below. Press. Make 8 blocks.

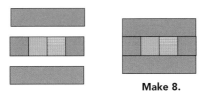

Make 8.

Purple block

5. Sew the turquoise strip from Step 2 to the purple edge of the other strip set from Step 1 so that both outer edges are turquoise. Press. Cut the strip set into eight 2½˝ sections.

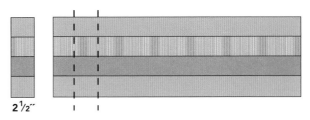

2½˝

Cut into 8 sections.

6. Sew 2 turquoise M rectangles to each section from Step 5 as shown below. Press. Make 8 blocks.

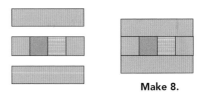

Make 8.

Turquoise block

Close-up of rectangle

Design

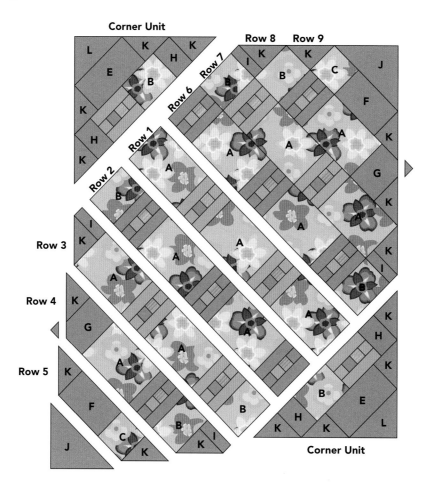

Quilt assembly diagram

It is very important that you lay out the design properly. Note the lettering on the illustration for arranging the pieces. I highly recommend a design wall, but if you don't have one, you could lay the pieces on a bed or floor. The pieces are sewn into diagonal rows and then the rows are sewn together.

1. Lay out the design as shown in the quilt assembly diagram above. Be sure to note the lettered rectangles and triangles on the diagram and match the lettered pieces you have cut with the diagram.

2. Start by assembling the upper left and lower right triangular corner units. Sew the blocks together into rows. Then join the longest rows together and add the corner triangles last. Place these units on the design wall.

3. In the center section, sew the floral focus fabric A rectangles to the adjoining purple or turquoise blocks in all of the rows. Press toward the large rectangles. Replace them on the design wall.

4. Join the I and K pieces together in rows 3, 4, 7, and 8. Replace them on the design wall.

5. Sew each diagonal row (1–9) as shown. In rows 4 and 8, trim the G rectangles even with the K triangle as shown. Sew rows 1, 2, 3, 4, and 5 together. Then sew rows 6, 7, 8, and 9 together. Next join these 2 sections together. Last, add the J triangles to the sides of rows 5 and 9 as shown in the diagram.

6. Join the corner sections from Step 2 to the quilt center. Press.

Optional Extras

I thought it would be interesting to add some Four-Patch blocks to the large purple corners of my quilt.

1. To do this, cut 8 squares $2\frac{1}{2}'' \times 2\frac{1}{2}''$ from the striped fabric and 4 squares $2\frac{1}{2}'' \times 2\frac{1}{2}''$ from each of the turquoise and floral fabrics. Stitch these squares together into Four Patches, using 2 striped, 1 turquoise, and 1 floral square in each Four-Patch set. Press the seams of each block open to make the block lie flat; then iron under a $\frac{1}{4}''$ seam allowance on each edge. Make 4 blocks.

Make 4.

2. Appliqué the Four-Patch blocks to the quilt using your favorite method. I machine appliquéd my blocks by sewing a small straight stitch right along the folded edge of each block (see full quilt photo, page 23).

BLOOMING RECTANGLES

Island Delight, 52″ × 62″, Judy Sisneros, 2007.

This project features a large rectangle surrounded by smaller rectangles, creating a fun and easy design. Start with a fabric you love, such as the floral shown here, and choose three companion fabrics. One should highlight a color in the focus fabric (such as the red), and the other two should blend with the focus fabric (the green and the fern). The small rectangles of red bloom around the floral center. There are 21 vertical rows. Using a design wall will really help you put this quilt together.

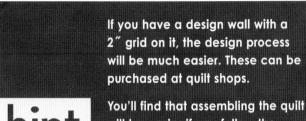

Fabric Requirements

(Yardage is based on 42″-wide fabric.)

FLORAL FOCUS FABRIC: 2 yards for rectangles and outer border

GREEN: 1¼ yards for inner border, rectangles, and binding

RED: 1 yard for inner border and rectangles

FERN PRINT: ⅞ yard for rectangles

BACKING: 3¼ yards

BATTING: 58″ × 68″

FUSIBLE WEB: ½ yard, 18″-wide

Cutting Instructions

(wof = width of fabric)

FROM THE FLORAL FOCUS FABRIC, CUT:

1 strip 20″ × wof. Be sure to include the area you want featured in the large rectangle.

Subcut into:

1 large **vertical** rectangle 12½″ × 18½″

8 vertical strips 2½″ × 20″. Cut these strips to feature any part of the design you choose, cutting 4 of the strips from one design area and 4 from another area.

9 strips 4½″ × wof

Cut 4 strips side-by-side.

FROM THE GREEN FABRIC, CUT:

3 strips 4½″ × wof

8 strips 2½″ × wof

Subcut 2 strips into:

2 strips 2½″ × 24½″

2 strips 2½″ × 14½″

Save the remaining 6 strips for the binding.

FROM THE RED FABRIC, CUT:

3 strips 4½″ × wof

Subcut 2 strips into:

26 rectangles 2½″ × 4½″

8 strips 1½″ × wof

Subcut 2 strips into:

2 strips 1½″ × 18½″

2 strips 1½″ × 14½″

Save the remaining 6 strips for the inner borders.

FROM THE FERN PRINT FABRIC, CUT:

3 strips 4½″ × wof

3 strips 2½″ × wof

Inner Border Around Large Rectangle

1. Sew a $1\frac{1}{2}'' \times 18\frac{1}{2}''$ red strip to each side of the large vertical rectangle. Press toward the red strips.

2. Sew the long edges of a $1\frac{1}{2}'' \times 14\frac{1}{2}''$ red strip and a $2\frac{1}{2}'' \times 14\frac{1}{2}''$ green strip together. Press toward the green strip. Sew 1 of these units to the top and the bottom of the large rectangle, noting the color placement. Press toward the red strips.

3. Sew a $2\frac{1}{2}'' \times 24\frac{1}{2}''$ green strip to each side of the central rectangle. Press toward the green strips.

4. Place the bordered rectangle on your design wall and refer to the quilt assembly diagram as you make the rest of the quilt.

Vertical Rows

SECTION ABOVE AND BELOW CENTER RECTANGLE

1. Sew $4\frac{1}{2}'' \times$ wof strips of 4 fabrics together, side-by-side, in the order **floral, red, fern, green**. Press. Trim selvages. Cut the strip set into $2\frac{1}{2}''$ sections. You should get 16 cuts, each measuring $2\frac{1}{2}'' \times 16\frac{1}{2}''$.

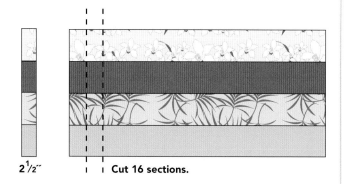

$2\frac{1}{2}''$ **Cut 16 sections.**

2. Place these sections on the design wall with the **floral** fabric touching the rectangle border in rows 7, 9, 11, 13, and 15. Do this on both the top and the bottom of the rectangle as shown in the assembly diagram.

3. Place the additional sections in rows 8, 10, 12, and 14 with the **green** rectangle overlapping the border by about half the green rectangle. This process takes 18 units, so you will need to make 2 more later when you are working in the *Small Rectangles* section (page 31). For now, just leave these on your design wall. The top and bottom edges will be uneven, but you'll trim them later.

hint When arranging and sewing the rows together, you can eyeball the placement of the overlapping rectangles. They do not have to be **perfectly** centered.

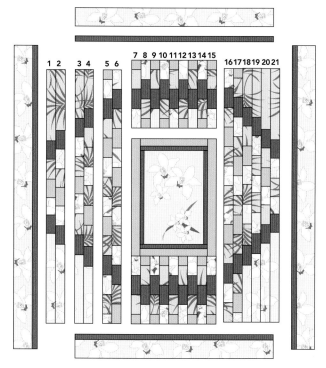

Quilt assembly diagram

SIDE SECTIONS

FLORAL CORNERS

1. Lay out the floral vertical $2\frac{1}{2}'' \times 20''$ strips side-by-side on a cutting mat so that the design pattern is connected. You'll have 2 sets of 4 related strips.

2. From the first set, trim the **top** of each strip to make the following lengths: row 1, 18½″; row 2, 16½″, row 3, 14½″; row 4, 12½″. From the second set, trim from the **top** of each strip to make the following lengths: row 21, 18½″: row 20, 16½″; row 19, 14½″; and row 18, 12½″. Place trimmed strips on the design wall in the lower corners as shown in the quilt assembly diagram.

Cut floral strips for lower left corner.

FERN CORNERS

Cut the fern 2½″ strips for the upper corners. You don't need to connect the pattern design in these strips. Make the following lengths: 14½″ for rows 1 and 21; 12½″ for rows 2 and 20; 10½″ for rows 3 and 19; and 8½″ for rows 4 and 18. Place these strips on your design wall in the upper corners.

SMALL RECTANGLES

1. Sew together 4½″ strips of **floral**, **green**, and **fern** side-by-side. Cut the strip set into units 2½″ × 12½″.

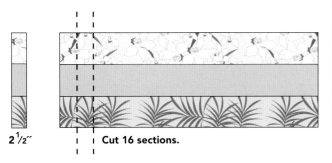

2½″   **Cut 16 sections.**

2. Sew together 4½″ strips of **green, floral**, and **fern** side-by-side. Cut the strip set into units 2½″ × 12½″.

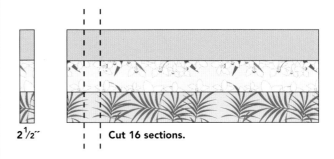

2½″   **Cut 16 sections.**

3. Sew a red 2½″ × 4½″ rectangle to one end of 4 of the **floral/green/fern** units and 4 of the **green/floral/fern** units as shown. Place the units on the design wall as shown in the quilt assembly diagram.

Make 4.

Make 4.

4. On your design wall, you now have the quilt center section (except for the 2 rows you are about to make) and the 4 outside corner sections. Except for the structured design of the red rectangles, the remainder of the side sections is very scrappy. Arrange the sections that you made in Steps 1–3 and the remaining red 2½″ × 4½″ rectangles to fill in the side sections.

5. Complete the last 2 rows above or below the center rectangle. You will have to take some sections apart to get the exact count in each row and the color arrangement that you like. When you are pleased with the layout, sew each vertical row.

Sewing the Rows Together

Once you have arranged and sewn the vertical rows, it's easy to finish sewing the quilt.

1. Sew rows 7–15 together to complete each section above and below the center rectangle. Press after sewing each row. Once the sections are together, trim the excess half-rectangles. Sew the sections to the top and bottom of the center rectangle. Press toward the borders.

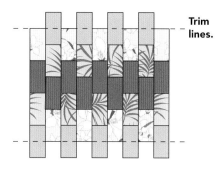

Trim excess half-rectangles.

2. Now sew the outside vertical sections. Join the rows in pairs—rows 1 and 2, rows 3 and 4, and so on. Press after sewing each pair. Join all the pairs together in each side section; then sew the sections to the quilt center and press. Trim the top and bottom of the rows evenly.

Outer Border

1. The quilt should measure $42\frac{1}{2}$″ × $52\frac{1}{2}$″ at this point. Before making the border, measure the quilt horizontally through the top, bottom, and center. The measurements should be the same. If not, trim as needed. Do the same vertically, measuring each side and the middle. Trim as needed.

2. Piece red $1\frac{1}{2}$″ inner border strips as needed to give you 2 pieces $1\frac{1}{2}$″ × $42\frac{1}{2}$″. Press the seams open so that the joined pieces lie flat.

3. Piece floral $4\frac{1}{2}$″ border strips together as needed to give you 2 pieces $4\frac{1}{2}$″ × $42\frac{1}{2}$″. Press the seams open.

4. Sew a red strip from Step 2 to a floral strip from Step 3. Press toward the floral strip. Repeat with the other 2 strips. Sew these to the top and bottom of the quilt. Press.

5. Piece red $1\frac{1}{2}$″ inner border strips together as needed to cut two $1\frac{1}{2}$″ × $62\frac{1}{2}$″ pieces. Press the seams open. Sew floral $4\frac{1}{2}$″ border strips together as needed to cut two $4\frac{1}{2}$″ × $62\frac{1}{2}$″ pieces. Sew the red border pieces to the floral border pieces. Press.

6. Sew the border units to the sides of the quilt. Press.

Optional Extras

I thought it would be fun to add some red rectangles to the border of the quilt. To do this, use fusible web (such as Steam-A-Seam 2). Following the manufacturer's instructions, fuse webbing to a piece of red fabric measuring at least 26″ × 3″. Cut 6 red rectangles 2″ × 4″ and fuse them to the border.

Detail of border appliqué

I also fused a few flowers from the floral fabric and added them to the quilt so that they extended into the green inner border.

Fused flowers

RECTANGLES BEHIND BARS

I Never Promised You a Rose Garden, 38″ × 50″, Judy Sisneros, 2007.

Want to try something a little different? Start with a large-scale print, create a peek-a-boo design and then combine it with Card Trick blocks to make a creative and fun wallhanging.

Fabric Requirements

(Yardage is based on 42″-wide fabric.)

FLORAL FOCUS FABRIC: 1¾ yards

GREEN: 1½ yards for Card Trick blocks, border, and binding

LIGHT PRINT: ⅔ yard for Card Trick blocks

BRIGHT GREEN: ½ yard for inserted bars

PINK: ¼ yard for border around center strip sections

BACKING: 1½ yards *if your fabric is not wide enough, you may need an additional yard

BATTING: 44″ × 56″

Cutting Instructions

(wof = width of fabric)

FROM THE FLORAL FOCUS FABRIC, CUT:

2 strips 12″ × wof, centering the design you want to feature. Cut each strip from a different part of the fabric. Each strip provides more than enough for a strip set.

note This strip set is the finished unit with bars between strips of focus fabric.

2 strips 4⅞″ × wof

Subcut into:

15 squares 4⅞″ × 4⅞″; then cut each square diagonally once for 30 triangles.

Cut diagonally once.

1 strip 5¼″ × wof

Subcut into:

4 squares 5¼″ × 5¼″; then cut each square diagonally twice for 16 triangles.

Cut diagonally twice.

FROM THE GREEN FABRIC, CUT:

2 strips 4⅞″ × wof

Subcut into:

11 squares 4⅞″ × 4⅞″; then cut each square diagonally once for 22 triangles.

1 strip 5¼″ × wof

Subcut into:

6 squares 5¼″ × 5¼″; then cut each square diagonally twice for 24 triangles.

5 strips 3½″ × wof (for border)

5 strips 2½″ × wof (for binding)

FROM THE LIGHT PRINT FABRIC, CUT:

1 strip 4⅞″ × wof

Subcut into:

6 squares 4⅞″ × 4⅞″; then cut each square diagonally once for 12 triangles.

2 strips 5¼″ × wof

Subcut into:

10 squares 5¼″ × 5¼″; then cut each square diagonally twice for 40 triangles.

FROM THE BRIGHT GREEN FABRIC, CUT:

1 strip 12″ × wof

Subcut into:

16 pieces 1¼″ × 12″

FROM THE PINK FABRIC, CUT:

4 strips 1¼″ × wof

Subcut into:

4 pieces 1¼″ × 24½″

4 pieces 1¼″ × 12″

Making the Large Rectangles With Bars

1. Position one 12″ × wof focus fabric strip, lengthwise, on the cutting mat. Start on the left side and cut a vertical piece 3″ × 12″. Place the vertical piece on the design wall.

   Next, cut a $1/2″ × 12″$ strip. Discard this narrow piece. Cut another vertical strip, varying the width from $1^3/4″$ to 3″, and place it on the design wall. Cut another $1/2″ × 12″$ strip and discard. Continue to cut a varying-width strip and then a consistent $1/2″$ strip until you have about 9 wider strips. Keep the varying vertical strips on the design wall so you don't lose track of the order.

   note — As you cut strips from the focus fabric, try to keep important parts of the fabric design showing, such as eyes if you are using an animal print.

Discard $1/2″$ strips between the larger strips.

2. On the design wall, place bright green $1^1/4″ × 12″$ strips between the floral strips from Step 1. Sew the floral and bright green strips together and press carefully toward the green bars, making sure there are no puckers. Measure the width of the strip set. Stop adding strips when the finished strip set is 23″ wide. You may need to trim the end pieces for an exact 23″. Using wider floral strips at each end allows room for any necessary trimming.

3. Repeat Steps 1 and 2 to make another strip set 12″ × 23″ from the second 12″ × wof floral strip. Be sure to make each strip set different, both in the width of each strip and in the fabric design featured. The same flower or animal should not be in the same place in each strip set.

4. Sew a $1^1/4″ × 12″$ piece of narrow pink border to each end of both strip sets. Press toward the narrow border.

5. Carefully trim the strip sets to 11″ high. Each unit should now measure 11″ × $24^1/2″$.

6. Sew a $1^1/4″ × 24^1/2″$ piece of narrow pink border to the top and bottom of each unit. Press toward the border. Place the bordered units on your design wall.

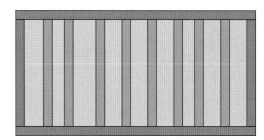

Rectangle behind bars, $24^1/2″ × 12^1/2″$

Making the Blocks

The blocks used in this quilt are based on traditional Card Trick blocks. After you have made the blocks, you will be able to create the design. Chain piece the units, making 1 set at a time. You need the number of blocks shown below.

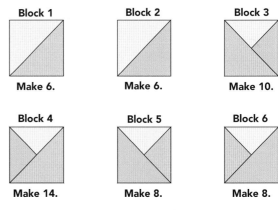

Numbers of blocks needed

1. Sew 1 set of blocks at a time. For example, make 6 of Block 1. Then make Block 2. Label your blocks to help with the design layout.

2. When sewing the blocks, first sew the small triangles together. Begin sewing at the 90° angle, not at the point. Chain piece as many as you need for each type of block. Press.

3. After the small triangles are sewn, sew each set to the appropriate large triangle to make the necessary number of each block.

4. Arrange the finished blocks on the design wall around the strip sets as shown in the quilt assembly diagram below.

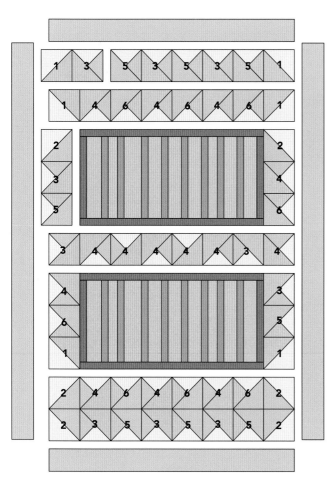

Quilt assembly diagram

Sewing the Units Together

1. Once all the pieces of the design have been made, sew each row together by first sewing the blocks in pairs. After all the blocks have been sewn together, press the seams open. Because of the thickness of the various seams, the quilt will lie flatter if the seams are pressed open. Then join the pairs into a row. Press.

2. Sew the top 2 rows together and then the bottom 2 rows. Place the rows on the design wall so you don't get confused.

3. Sew the center row together and place it on the design wall.

4. Sew the vertical side rows together for each rectangle and sew them to the sides of the rectangles. Place the units on the design wall.

5. Finish sewing the quilt rows together. Press carefully.

Border

1. Cut 2 of the green 3½″ border strips to measure 32½″. Sew the strips to the top and bottom of the quilt.

2. Cut a green 3½″ border strip in half. Remove the selvages and sew each half strip to a remaining border strip. Cut each long strip to measure 50½″. Sew one of these strips to each side of the quilt. Press.

FINISHING

FOLLOWING ARE A FEW SUGGESTIONS FOR FINISHING YOUR QUILT.

Batting

I usually use all-cotton batting in my quilts. It is thin, flat, and easy to machine quilt. If you are making a wallhanging, it will lie flatter if you use all-cotton batting. You may also use a thin cotton-polyester batting. Wool batting is excellent, but quite a bit more expensive.

Backing

I suggest you use a printed fabric containing colors that blend with the quilt. If you use a solid fabric, all your machine quilting will show up on the back. If you are a beginner at machine quilting, you will like a print because it will disguise less-than-perfect stitches. Do not use a cotton-polyester blend fabric on the back of an all-cotton quilt.

If your quilt measures more than 40″ wide, you will need to piece the backing. Be sure to remove the selvages before piecing the backing. If working out of your stash, you may need to piece more than one fabric. If you piece the backing, do not just sew a piece on the edge or insert a strip in the center. That makes it look as if you didn't have enough fabric. Arrange the fabrics in a pleasing manner and sew them together or piece them off-center and call it "back art."

Lay the quilt backing wrong side up on a flat surface, place the batting on top, and smooth out any wrinkles. Add the pressed quilt top and baste with thread for hand quilting or rustproof safety pins for machine quilting.

Quilting

If you are a beginner, it's a good idea to buy a book on quilting or take a beginning quilting class at a local quilt shop. All of the quilts in this book are machine quilted because it is a much quicker way to complete the quilt. Of course, you may hand quilt if you prefer.

Free-motion quilting looks great on these quilts. Follow the larger designs or simply make large leaves, flowers, stars, or stippling. Quilt the body of the quilt first, starting in the center, and then the borders. Stitch in-the-ditch (along seamlines) between the quilt and the borders and between the inner and outer borders. Always be sure to quilt in the border, even if you do just a couple of straight lines. If the quilt is quilted and the border is not, it will not lie flat!

Binding

These instructions are for double-fold straight-grain binding (also called French fold binding). It will finish a scant ½″ wide.

1. Trim excess batting and backing from the quilt.

2. Cut binding strips 2½″ wide; you will need enough to go around the sides of the quilt plus 12″. Piece the strips together with diagonal seams to make a continuous binding strip. Press the seams open; then press the entire strip in half lengthwise with wrong sides together.

3. With raw edges even, pin the binding to the edge of the quilt, starting a few inches from a corner. Leave the first few inches of the binding unattached. Start sewing, using a ¼″ seam allowance.

4. Stop ¼″ away from the first corner as shown; backstitch one stitch. Lift the presser foot and needle. Rotate the quilt one quarter turn. Fold the binding at a right angle so it extends straight above the quilt. Then bring the binding strip down even with the next edge of the quilt. Begin sewing at the folded edge. Repeat in the same manner at all corners.

Stitch to ¼″ from the corner.

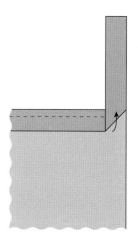

First fold for miter

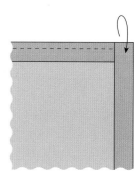

Second fold alignment

5. When you reach the last side, fold under the beginning end of the binding strip ¼″. Lay the end of the binding strip over the beginning folded edge. Continue stitching beyond the folded edge. Trim the excess binding. Fold the binding over the raw edges to the quilt back and hand stitch, mitering the corners.

GALLERY

IT'S ALWAYS FUN to see variations of a project quilt. Following are some of those variations. All quilts were made by me, except as noted.

More Than Lavender

54″ × 72″, Judy Sisneros, 2003.

Garden Party

54″ × 72″, Judy Sisneros, 2003.

Surfer's Delight

72″ × 96″, Judy Sisneros, 2005. Owned by Brennan Keller.
This twin-size quilt looks wonderful on my grandson's bed.

Alyson's Aloha

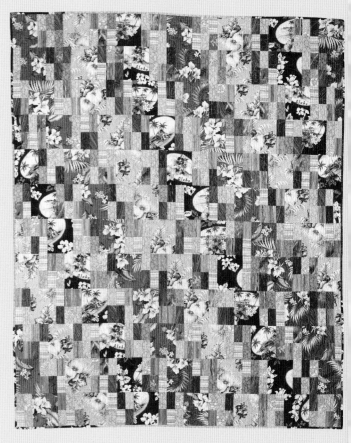

78″ × 96″, Judy Sisneros, 2004. Owned by Alyson Keller. This quilt fits
on my granddaughter Alyson's double bed. We found grass skirt
dust ruffles for both grandchildren's beds.

Butterfly Garden

$32^1/2$″ × $38^1/2$″, Ruth Breunig, Los Alamitos, California, 2006.

Flaming Iris

96″ × 104″, Judy Sisneros, 2006. Owned by Donna and Garrett Earle.
The cutouts in the bottom corners make this quilt fit perfectly around
the bedposts on my daughter's queen-size bed.

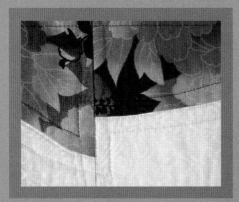

Geisha

42″ × 48″, Judy Sisneros, 2002.

Wisteria in Bloom

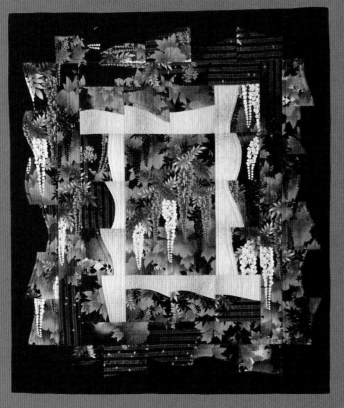

42″ × 48″, Judy Sisneros, 2003.

Spanish Rose

36″ × 42″, Judy Sisneros, 2004.

Cranes in Flight

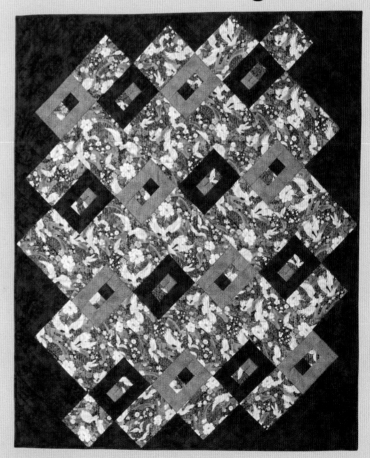

54″ × 66″, Judy Sisneros, 2007.

Chicken Coop

38″ × 46″, Judy Sisneros, 2000.

Wolves

32″ × 52″, Judy Sisneros, 2000.

Tropical

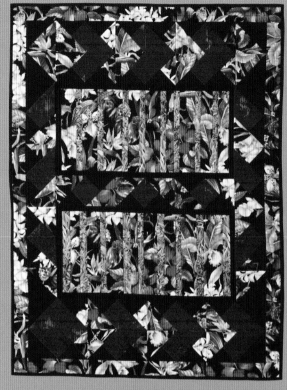

36″ × 48″, Judy Sisneros, 2003.

Jungle Fever

32″ × 43″, Patti Henderson, Auburn, California, 2007.

Sunflowers in My Garden

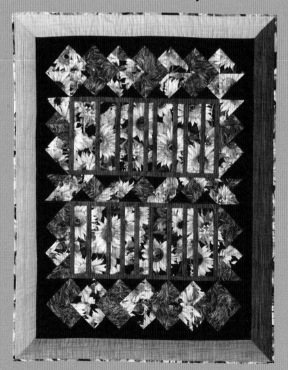

41″ × 53″, Kathy Sanchez, Grass Valley, California, 2007.

ABOUT THE AUTHOR

Photo by Ronald D. Burris

Judy Sisneros's first memory of sewing is making a rag doll and doll clothes as a child. She took her first sewing lessons in 1964 but didn't start quilting until 1987. Her first quilting lessons were through the local adult school.

After a move to California's far north coast, she began making landscape quilts. Her first book, *Simply Landscapes*, was published in 1994. Her second book, the popular 9-*Patch Pizzazz: Fast, Fun & Finished in a Day*, was published by C&T Publishing in 2006. Judy loves teaching and feels fortunate to be making a living doing something she loves.

Judy tries to add a new workshop every year because so many of her students are repeat customers. She is available to teach and lecture nationwide. Her love of people, travel, and fabric makes her an enthusiastic teacher! Kits are available for purchase. Visit her website at www.judysisneros.com.

Judy has three grown children and seven grandchildren. She lives in Rocklin, California, near Sacramento.

RESOURCES

Fabric kits for some of the projects in this book are available through www.judysisneros.com.

For a list of other fine books from C&T Publishing, ask for a free catalog:

C&T Publishing, Inc.
P.O. Box 1456
Lafayette, CA 94549
(800) 284-1114
Email: ctinfo@ctpub.com
Website: www.ctpub.com

For quilting supplies:

Cotton Patch
1025 Brown Ave.
Lafayette, CA 94549
(800) 835-4418 or
(925) 283-7883
Email: CottonPa@aol.com
Website: www.quiltusa.com

C&T Publishing's professional photography is now available to the public. Visit us at www.ctmediaservices.com.

NOTE: Because fabric manufacturers keep fabrics in print for only a short time, fabrics used in the quilts shown may not be currently available.

Benartex
1359 Broadway, Suite 1100
New York, NY 10018
(212) 840-3250
Email: info@benartex.com

Fairfield Processing (Batting)
P.O. Box 1130
Danbury, CT 06813
(800) 980-8000
Email: info@poly-fil.com

Kona Bay Fabrics
1637 Kahai Street
Honolulu, HI 96819
(800) 531-7913
Email: konabay@konabay.com

Michael Miller Fabrics
118 West 22nd Street, 5th Floor
New York, NY 10011
(212) 704-0774
Email: info@michaelmillerfabrics.com

Olfa
5500 North Pearl Street, Suite 400
Rosemont, IL 60018
(800) 962-6532

Superior Threads
87 East 2580 South
St. George, UT 84790
(800) 499-1777
Email: info@superiorthreads.com

Trendtex Fabrics
(808) 842-1356
Email: trendtex@mac.com

GREAT TITLES FROM

C&T PUBLISHING

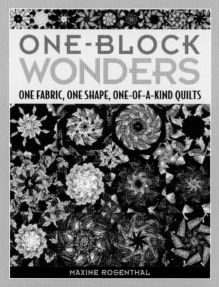

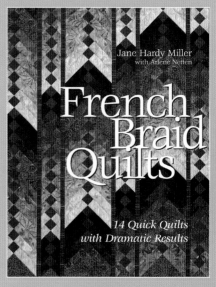

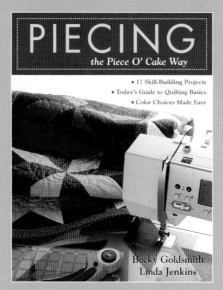

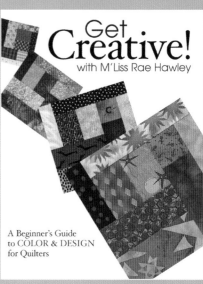